HOMEWARD BOUND

ELLIOTT HAYES

Playwrights Canada Press
Toronto

Homeward Bound © Copyright 1991 Elliott Hayes
Foreword to *Homeward Bound* © Copywright 1991 Margaret Atwood

Playwrights Canada Press is the publishing imprint of
the Playwrights Union of Canada: 54 Wolseley St., 2nd fl.
Toronto, Ontario CANADA
M5T 1A5
Tel. (416) 947-0201 Fax. (416) 947-0159

Playwrights Canada Press operates with the generous assistance of
The Canada Council - Writing and Publishing Section, and Theatre Section,
and the Ontario Arts Council.

Front cover photo by Tom Skudra.   *Edited and designed by Tony Hamill.*

Canadian Cataloguing in Publication Data
Elliott Hayes, 1956-
        Homeward bound
A play
ISBN 0-88754-485-1
I. Title.
PS8565.A93H66 1992   C812'.54   C92-094693-3
PR9199.3.H39H66 1992

First edition: September 1992
Printed and bound in Canada.

To my family, with special thanks to Marti Maraden and David William.

FOREWORD

by Margaret Atwood

Elliott Hayes' new play is a comedy of manners, but with a difference: comedies of manners used to be about love, but this is the late Twentieth Century, and *Homeward Bound* is a comedy about death.

The machine that winds it up and keeps it going is simple, though outrageous: Bonnie amd Glen, two acutely square and respectble middle-aged parents, have thrown a family dinner for their two children and their respective mates, to announce — as it turns out — that Glen is dying of an incurable disease and intends to kill himself as a sort of *pousse-café* to the meal. The travel brochures which Bonnie is so scattily examining in the opening scene gather much darker connotations by the closing one: they represent what Bonnie intends to do with the remainder of her life, afterwards.

Homeward Bound is a play that pulls the term "comedy of manners" inside out. For example, one of the most immediately obvious things about its characters is their lack of manners, in the usual sense of the word. Their insistence on not listening to one another, their fiercely-honed skills of contradiction, incomprehension and interruption, and their peevish cries of "What?" and "What do you mean?" are strewn over the surface of their supposedly normal, supposedly suburban social life like booby-traps.

Perhaps the true subject of the play is not death, after all, but the booby-trap: the sensation of a presumably solid ground exploding suddenly beneath our feet. Even the titles of the play becomes suspect: "homeward bound", which strikes us at first as a line from one of those cheerful, healthy nineteenth-century sea-chanties of the *"Yo-ho, my lads, and we'll be homeward bound"* variety, disintegrates in the light of the plot. That cosy and comforting word "homeward" splits into its components — "home," as in "mental" and "ward", as in hospital — and "bound" takes on sinister overtones of shackles. The characters in the play find themselves in — or help to create — a world in which logic is decidedly skewed, but from which they can't escape. Although *Homeward Bound* is scattered with domestic and even nostalgic references to toys and games — guessing games, the crossword puzzle that obsesses Glen, the Winnie-the-Pooh books that go hurtling through the air in the play's final moments — the game the play itself most closely resembles is a game of *Snakes and Ladders*, with a great many snakes and hardly any ladders at all.

Although *Homeward Bound* owes something to Pinter — with its skipped middle terms and its conversational cross-purposes, something to Chekov — with its relentless examination of middle-class facade and ennui, and something to Oscar Wilde — lines like, "if you're going to take your parents' deaths personally, you are going to be very unhappy" are almost pure Wilde; the malaise it chiefly explores is an exceedingly contemporary one. Wilde got many of his best comic effects by reversing the terms of conventional aphorisms, but the problem at heart of *Homeward Bound* is the dissolution of convention itself. How do you navigate if all the channel markers, maps and even stars have disappeared?

Hayes' characters are living in the midst of the disorientation that results when all previously-accepted social conventions and values have been thrown into the blender. Bonnie's confusion about what to call her son's male lover — she comes up with "combine" — is symptomatic of a general problem. It's no accident that the play opens with the word Tibet and ends with talk of Pharoahs and Suttee.

Worse: these characters are living at a time in which language itself is losing its ability to signify. Many of them are connected, in some way, with communication: Nick is a reporter, Norris sells typewriters, Bonnie and Glen are addicted to word games. But their own grip on language — as an instrument for real communication, as the carrier of real meaning — is slipping badly. As usual, it's Bonnie — not exactly the herione of the play, but its core — who articulates this growing sense of inarticulateness:

> ...words start losing their sting at some point in time, you know...in your lifetime...In my lifetime too, for that matter...God knows when...but you see, our ability to feel anything is bound by our ability to

express it and my talking about it sounds muddy
because my thoughts are muddy and my thoughts
are muddy because I can't see what I mean.

Because we don't think the way we used to,
anymore. None of us do. We just don't.

Out of this dark-enough material, Elliott Hayes has fashioned a
brisk, intricate, deranging and tightly-strung play with, oddly, a lot of
laughter in it. Aftr all, it is a comedy of manners, of a sort. But the
laughter is nervous laughter, interspersed with cringes. If art is a mirror,
Elliott Hayes' art is a funhouse mirror, and what we see in it is
fragments of ourselves: distorted, grotesque even, but recognizable. The
home we are bound for, or to, is our own.

Author's Note

The first reading reveals a great deal about the musical nature of the play. The timing essentially dictates itself, particularily when two, or more, conversations seem to be going on at the same time.

Given the subject matter, one may be seduced into beoming sentimental, but the play can't take that. The language is precise and the dialogue is unabashedly epigrammatic in places, so have fun with it. It's also worth noting that *Homeward Bound* observes the unities and that the effect of the play is cumulative. In fact, a great deal is unresolved and no one voice is "authoritative". Of course, Bonnie seems to have the complete picture, but even she is caught up by events in the end.

The Characters

The Family
Nick Beacham...................35
Norris Beacham-Spanner.....38
Bonnie Beacham................65

Glen Beacham............68
The Sons-in-Law
Guy Thompson..........38
Kevin Spanner...........35

Notes on the characters

GLEN is a straightforward retired lawyer, who seems to have found a way to disengage from the outrageous behaviour of his family, but he is certainly not without a sense of humour. In one production he used a walkman at one point, in another production he was always at work on the crossword puzzle. The choice is yours.

BONNIE is someone who loves words and who loves getting to the bottom of everyhting. She amuses herself, does not consider "middle class" a pejorative at all, and knows what's what, even if she operates according to her own "Bonnie's logic". Death is a good, almost cheerful thing — until it happens.

NICK is probably a bon vivant juggling too many balls in the air. He drinks too much, but is not yet an alcoholic; a fine distinction he obviously won't be able to argue with Guy anymore. Nick is also the favoured child, as Norris is all too aware. He is a reporter, and used to listening — to advantage.

NORRIS states her raison d'être: "the only reason I tell people what to do is because I know what they should do." Nevertheless, you can never forget that Norris is doing her best. She doesn't want her family to know her troubles. It's a fine line, and cast members will make fun of you, but Norris can never simply be a bitch. Love her.

KEVIN knows what the family thinks of him. He's an all-round guy who has learned a rather devastating thing about his wife. The key to his scene with Nick is that he's desperate to hear what he wants to hear and doesn't take time to analyse what is being said.

GUY is a talented, shy, sweet-tempered alcoholic. He is finally coming to terms with that and thinks that confession is a good thing — tonight. Nick and Guy have yet to deal with the hard facts about drinking, and Nick certainly has the perfect excuse not to tell his parents about the Alcoholics Anonymous meeting — tonight.

The Time: evening.

The Place: the suburbs.

Homeward Bound had its world premiere at The Stratford Festival, Ontario, Canada, July 1991, with the following cast:

BONNIE	*Barbara Bryne*
GLEN	*Douglas Rain*
NICK	*Tom Wood*
NORRIS	*Michelle Fisk*
KEVIN	*Miles Potter*
GUY	*Peter Donalldson*

Directed by Marti Maraden.
Designed by Patrick Clark.
Lighting design by James Milburn.
Sound design by Keith Handegord.
Stage manager — Ann Stuart.

Homeward Bound had its American premiere at Theatre Three, Dallas, Texas, January 1992, with the following cast:

BONNIE	*Esther Benson*
GLEN	*Jerry Haynes*
NICK	*Artie Olaisen*
NORRIS	*Connie Nelson*
KEVIN	*Jerry Crow*
GUY	*Bill Jenkins*

Directed by Norman Young.
Associate director/production stage manager — Lawrence O'Dwyer.
Scenic & sound design by Tritan Wilson.
Costume design by Rick Tankersley.
Lighting design by Linda Blase.

Act One

A livingroom. A family, after dinner.
GLEN is sitting in a comfortable chair,
doing the evening's crossword. BONNIE
is reading travel brochures.

BONNIE   Tibet, Glen?

GLEN   No.

BONNIE   Where then?

GLEN   Nowhere.

                        Pause.

BONNIE   Which is worse? Suicide or murder?

GLEN   Murder.

BONNIE   Do you *really* think so?

GLEN   Murder.

BONNIE   Why?

GLEN   Murder is something you do to someone else.

BONNIE   Well what about suicide? Think about all the
                      people you leave behind. Aren't you doing
                      something to them?

GLEN   Bonnie, we've been through all this.

BONNIE   I know, but I keep flip-flopping in my head. I
                can't help thinking some of the time that suicide
                is the worst...but then I think about killing
                someone and I think, oh no, I'm going to go to
                jail. And maybe I'm going to spend years on
                death row,waiting for a reprieve and being pushed
                around by lesbians with tattoos and things and I
                get so tense that I think maybe I should kill
                myself and get it over with.

                            Pause.

BONNIE   Is that why murder is worse? Because you're
                alive?

                            NICK *enters and pours himself a*
                            brandy.

NICK   What are you two talking about?

GLEN   Nothing.

BONNIE   Nothing. Just chatting.

NICK   Great dinner.

GLEN   Yes, it was.

BONNIE   Thank you. It's so nice to get compliments on a
                roast these days. And a rare one, no less.People
                don't even call it a roast anymore, do they?

NICK   What do you mean?

BONNIE   Norris called it red meat.

GLEN   It is.

BONNIE   It sounds derogatory.

GLEN   She ate it, didn't she?

BONNIE   (*beat, then trying to say it different ways*) *Red* meat. Red *meat*. Red-meat.

GLEN   Stop that. Please.

BONNIE   (*pausing*) Things always seem so complete after a big dinner. Don't you think? And it's not because you've solved anything that's wrong with the world or anything, but because you've had enough of it. You've eaten enough. You've drunk enough. And you've talked enough. You've dealt with the world, without really listening to what other people have to say. And then you've put it to bed. Washed it up with the dishes. Put the world out with the cat. Don't you think?

GLEN   What?

BONNIE   (*to* NICK) See?

NICK   See what?

BONNIE   Contentment.

NICK   Are you content, dad?

GLEN   What?

BONNIE   See?

NICK   Is that contentment?

BONNIE   It's too bad Guy couldn't make it.

NICK   I told you. He'll be here later. He had to work. Late.

BONNIE   I see. He'll be here later. For the champagne.

NICK   He said he would. What have you got up your sleeve, anyway?

BONNIE   You'll see.

NICK   What's the big secret?

BONNIE   (*ignoring the question*) What's Guy doing?

NICK   He's got an exhibition coming up.

BONNIE   You know, I was talking about you at bridge the other day and I started to talk about Guy, and I didn't know what to call him.

NICK   What do you mean?

BONNIE   What do you call him?

NICK   Guy. What should I call him?

BONNIE   Don't be sarcastic.

NICK   Sarcastic?

BONNIE   I know that removing the terms "husband"and "wife" and "Marriage" from your circumstances may have simplified your life, but it creates great complications for those of us who still have the convention entrenched in our brains. For some of us, you know, "husband and wife" are like "right and left" or "Light and dark". It may be "my problem", but it is still a problem.

NICK   What is the problem?

BONNIE   You need a new convention.

NICK   Why?

BONNIE   Mucking about with conventions makes people nervous.

NICK   I don't care.

BONNIE	Why not "combine." That's what we came up with at bridge.
GLEN	Combine?
NICK	That sounds like a piece of farm machinery.
GLEN	It is a piece of farm machinery.
BONNIE	If you want to be literal about it, I suppose it is. But we weren't trying to be literal, were we? We were looking for a new convention.
GLEN	Literalism is the curse of the middle class.
BONNIE	Who said that?
GLEN	I did.
BONNIE	Oh pooh. You can't quote yourself.
NICK	Guy is my "friend."
GLEN	Friend?
BONNIE	That only works if you say it funny. And besides, it only works properly if things are going well. It's not like "husband and wife." Those words can evoke a picture of living hell if you know the people involved.
GLEN	Kevin and Norris.
BONNIE	(*ignoring* GLEN) You'd have to stand on your head to make "friend" sound awful. Or grimace. Or point. And that wouldn't do, would it? Everyone would think there was something wrong with you, not with your (*making a face*) "friend."
NICK	I think, the point is...is that it's not conventional, and therefore there is no convention.

BONNIE   Oh?

NICK   It's just a...relationship.

BONNIE   But that doesn't solve the problem of what you call each other.

GLEN   Nick and Guy.

BONNIE   Or what other people call you.

NICK   Lover.

BONNIE   Oh no.

NICK   Oh no what?

BONNIE   That's worse than friend. It's too explicit.

NICK   Explicit?

BONNIE   It sounds like a verb. Love-er. The explicit is implicit. Besides, if you are in it for the long haul, there will be times when you may not love your lover any more than you feel friendly towards your friend. Trust me. You need a generic term.

NICK   Alright. My "better half".

BONNIE   Too sarcastic.

GLEN   (*to himself*) Chester Closetwood.

BONNIE   What?

GLEN   Chester Closetwood.

BONNIE   Why would they call each other Chester Closetwood?

GLEN   Cedar.

BONNIE   Cedar? What are you talking about?

GLEN   Cedar! (*shaking the newspaper*)

BONNIE   Cedar?

GLEN   (*articulating clearly*) Chest or Closet Wood.

BONNIE   Oh. (*laughing*) Cedar, of course.

NORRIS *enters.*

NORRIS   (*to* NICK) The twins are waiting for you, Nick.

NICK   What?

NORRIS   They're waiting for you.

NICK   What for?

NORRIS   Don't you want to read them a story?

NICK   No.

NORRIS   I told them you did.

NICK   Why did you tell them that?

NORRIS   I thought you would.

NICK   Well, I don't.

NORRIS   Please.

NICK   No.

NORRIS   You're horrible.

NICK   I'm sorry, I just don't want to.

NORRIS   (*to* Bonnie *and* Glen) Isn't he horrible?

NICK   I just don't want to read to the twins. O.K.?

NORRIS   But they're waiting for you.

NICK   They're only waiting for me because you told
                them I was coming.

NORRIS   I thought you would want to. (*pause*) They are
                your nephews after all.

NICK   Why can't Kevin read to them? He is their
                father, after all.

NORRIS   (*beat*) He doesn't like reading to them.

NICK   Neither do I.

NORRIS   How would you know? You never do!

NICK   I know I never do!

NORRIS   (*quickly*) Well, they're waiting for you anyway.

NICK   Norris!

NORRIS   If you don't go they'll come down here and get
                you, and you know they'll upset dad and he'll yell
                at them and they'll cry. And it will be all your
                fault.

NICK   I'm having a drink.

NORRIS   Well take it upstairs with you.

NICK   Won't that be setting a bad example?

NORRIS   Is it too much to ask you to put it down for ten
                minutes then?

NICK   Yes.

NORRIS   You still have to go up.

NICK	Christ.
NORRIS	You're going to upset them, if you don't.
GLEN	You'd better go.
NORRIS	What's that supposed to mean?
GLEN	Nothing.
NORRIS	Have you got something against your grandchildren?
BONNIE	Norris...
NORRIS	You're all horrible.
NICK	I'll go.
BONNIE	Thank you.
NORRIS	He's only going because I made him. You don't have to thank him.
NICK	What'll I read to them?
NORRIS	Nothing scary.
GLEN	Poe.
NORRIS	Is that supposed to be funny?
NICK	What do they like?
NORRIS	Ask them.
NICK	Do they have any picture books?
NORRIS	You can't read a picture book.
NICK	Yes you can.

NORRIS	You just don't want to read to them.
NICK	No. I don't. But that's already been put beside the point, hasn't it?
BONNIE	Read them *Zoom*.
NORRIS	That's too short.
NICK	What do you mean, it's too short?
NORRIS	There aren't enough words. I want you to be up there for a while. I want you to get to know them. I want them to get to know you.
NICK	Oh Christ.
BONNIE	But they love that book.
NORRIS	He's supposed to be *reading* to them.
NICK	Did they really ask for me, or did you put it in their heads?
GLEN	Read Poe.
NORRIS	Daddy!
BONNIE	I say read *Zoom*.
NORRIS	Read whatever you like!
NICK	I will.
NORRIS	Just don't scare them. They'll never sleep. And it's bad enough they have to share a room with us.

NICK *exits.*

NORRIS	You'd think he'd want to read to his nephews.
BONNIE	Did you ask him first?

NORRIS	No. Of course not.
BONNIE	Well?
NORRIS	Well what?
BONNIE	What do you expect?
NORRIS	I expect him to want to read to his nephews. He's had nothing to do with them since they were born, and I...I think it's time. I know I always wished I had an uncle who read to me. And took me to Europe. And all those things....Like that movie...only it was an aunt, of course. But it's the same thing. Only I don't want to be dead. Like in the movie. Being the mother, I mean.

Pause.

GLEN	Where's Kevin?
NORRIS	I don't know.
BONNIE	Wasn't he helping you with the dishes?
NORRIS	Yes.
GLEN	Is he still in the kitchen?
NORRIS	I don't know where he is! He went out.
GLEN	Out?
BONNIE	Out where?
NORRIS	Out the back door. I don't know.
GLEN	Did you have a fight?
NORRIS	No.
GLEN	Did you?

NORRIS   None of your business.

BONNIE   What about?

NORRIS   Nothing.

BONNIE   He was kind of quiet during dinner. Was it
                  something one of us said? He usually has
                  something to say about something. I mean, he
                  always has an opinion at least, whether or not he
                  knows what we're talking about.

NORRIS   He just went to get some fresh air.

BONNIE   Are you sure?

NORRIS   He went for a walk. (*strongly*) O.K.?

BONNIE   O.K.

GLEN   It's kind of cold for that, isn't it?

BONNIE   Glen.

GLEN   What?

BONNIE   Shut up, honey.

GLEN   What is it? What did I say?

BONNIE   Do your puzzle.

GLEN   I just said it was cold.

BONNIE   I know. But...

GLEN   But what?

NORRIS   Would you both please stop talking about me as
                  if I wasn't here. You're always doing that and it
                  always drives me crazy. I am standing right here
                  in the room.

GLEN   We're not talking about you.

BONNIE   We're talking about Kevin.

GLEN   And he's *not* here.

BONNIE   Glen.

GLEN   What?

BONNIE   Do your puzzle.

GLEN   Oh. O.K.

                    Pause.

NORRIS   What's your big secret?

BONNIE   You'll see.

NORRIS   Champagne?

BONNIE   You'll see.

NORRIS   It must have been expensive. It's French, isn't it?

BONNIE   Yes.

                    Pause.

NORRIS   The boys need a new pair of Reeboks. Did I tell
              you?

BONNIE   Yes.

                    Pause.

NORRIS   So. Where are you going?

GLEN   Nowhere.

BONNIE   I haven't decided yet. Somewhere old, though.
                Older than here. Tibet sort of appeals to me, but
                only in my head. I'm sure it stinks. The raw
                sewage, I mean. And I'd hate all the walking.
                And I can't abide curry. Still, its nice to talk
                about it as a possibility.

NORRIS   How about you, dad?

GLEN   Nowhere.

BONNIE   Betty Tyler wants to share a condo in Maui, but I
                can't imagine her at breakfast. She's bad enough
                at lunch.

NORRIS   How about Florida?

BONNIE   I want an old place. Not old people.

NORRIS   Mexico?

BONNIE   Been there.

NORRIS   Where haven't you been?

GLEN   Nowhere.

BONNIE   Everywhere on this table is where I have not
                been.

NORRIS   Well, if you want my opinion, I think Maui
                with Betty Tyler sounds nice. At least you'd be
                comfortable there. And you like pineapples,
                don't you? They have all sorts of pineapples
                there.

BONNIE   I am indifferent to pineapples.

                              Pause.

NORRIS   Need any help, dad?

GLEN   Nope.

                                    Pause.

NORRIS   Give me a clue.

GLEN   Um...

NORRIS   Come on. Just any clue.

BONNIE   Chester Closetwood.

NORRIS   What?

GLEN   I've already got it.

NORRIS   Got what?

BONNIE   Chester Closetwood.

NORRIS   What's that?

BONNIE   Cedar. (*laughing*)

NORRIS   Cedar?

GLEN   O.K. I've got one. Slimy substance.

NORRIS   How many letters?

GLEN   Four.

NORRIS   (*looking over his shoulder*) What's the number?

GLEN   I don't know.

NORRIS   Where is it?

GLEN   It's not in here.

NORRIS   What?

GLEN	You said just any old clue.
NORRIS	I meant in the puzzle.
GLEN	Oh.
NORRIS	So I could help you out.
GLEN	I don't want any help.
NORRIS	Well it's no fun just figuring out what word pops into your head.
BONNIE	Ooze.
NORRIS	What?
GLEN	How'd you know that?
NORRIS	Know what?
BONNIE	Because I know you.
GLEN	Too well.
NORRIS	What does she know too well?
GLEN	Ooze.
NORRIS	What?
BONNIE	His word. Slimy substance.
NORRIS	Oh.
BONNIE	Give me another.
NORRIS	I don't care what's in his head. I want to know what's in the paper.
GLEN	(*handing her the paper*) Here. (*to* BONNIE) Director Elia. Four letters. No, five.

BONNIE	Kazan. Too easy. *A Streetcar Named Desire* was on the late show last week.
NORRIS	This isn't fair.
BONNIE	What's not fair?
NORRIS	What you're playing.
BONNIE	You can play too.
GLEN	Child's train. Eight letters.
NORRIS	This is stupid.
BONNIE	What is it then?
NORRIS	(*irritated*) I don't know.
GLEN	It's not so stupid then, is it?
BONNIE	Eight letters?

NICK *enters.*

NORRIS	What are you doing here? You're supposed to be with the boys.
NICK	They were asleep.
NORRIS	I don't believe you.
NICK	They were both sound asleep.
NORRIS	They must have been pretending.
NICK	Then maybe they don't want me to read to them.
NORRIS	You just don't *want* to read to them.
NICK	Norris!

NORRIS	Do you?
NICK	What am I supposed to do? Wake them up so that I can read them a bedtime story so they can fall asleep?
NORRIS	Very funny.
NICK	I'll go right back up there and wake them up if you want me to.
GLEN	Please don't.
NICK	Hey boys, wake up, it's time to go to sleep.
NORRIS	They were only asleep because you took so long to go up.
NICK	You want me to wake them?
GLEN	No.
BONNIE	Choo Choo.
NICK	What?
BONNIE	That's two words though, isn't it?
NICK	What is?
NORRIS	It's just some stupid game that they're playing.
NICK	Choo choo?
GLEN	It's still eight letters.
BONNIE	Glen, really! That's cheating.
GLEN	O.K. Four-Four. That's still eight.
BONNIE	But I've already got it.
GLEN	So you win. So what?

NICK   Wins what? What do you win?

BONNIE   (*picking up a travel brochure*) How about a trip
                to Greece!

NICK   Are you going to Greece?

GLEN   No.

BONNIE   Yes.

NICK   When?

NORRIS   This is stupid.

NICK   What is?

BONNIE   Nick, will you get me a brandy?

GLEN   You drink too much.

BONNIE   Pooh.

NICK   (*to* Glen) Do you want one?

GLEN   No.

BONNIE   Give him a small one.

NICK   Norris?

NORRIS   (*pointedly*) No. Thanks. I had plenty of wine at
                dinner, thank you. Didn't you?

                        No one answers her. NICK *goes for*
                        drinks. GLEN *picks up the paper and*
                        resumes his crossword. BONNIE *opens*
                        the brochure from Greece.

NICK   Where's Kevin?

NORRIS   Out.

NICK	Out where?
NORRIS	I don't know.
NICK	(*to* Bonnie) Where'd he go?

BONNIE shrugs.

NORRIS	They don't know either.
NICK	Did you have a fight?
NORRIS	Why do you all think that we have to have a fight for Kevin to go for a walk and get some fresh air?
NICK	I notice you did not say you didn't.
BONNIE	Nick.
NICK	What?
BONNIE	We've already had this non-conversation once, while you were out of the room.
NICK	Oh.
NORRIS	Can we drop the subject of Kevin?
GLEN	Gladly.
NORRIS	(*quickly*) What's that supposed to mean?
GLEN	Nothing.
NORRIS	What's wrong with Kevin? Or should I say, what's wrong with Kevin tonight?
BONNIE	I thought we were dropping the subject?
NICK	We were.

GLEN	I thought we did.
NORRIS	We have.

Long pause.

NORRIS	What shall we talk about?

Everyone looks at her.

NORRIS	How's your cough, dad?
GLEN	Sedated.
NORRIS	Have they figured out what to do?
GLEN	Uh huh.
NORRIS	(*irritated*) And how was the conference in Vancouver, Nick? Any books worth reading this year?
NICK	It was wet.
NORRIS	Is that all?
NICK	(*shrugging*) It rained.
NORRIS	If you want to talk about the weather, will you at least talk about the weather here so that we can all talk about it.
NICK	Why do we have to talk about anything?
NORRIS	I asked you a question. All you have to do is answer it.
NICK	I did. It was wet.
NORRIS	That's not a real answer.
NICK	It is too.

NORRIS	What did you do there? Did you meet any famous authors?
NICK	This is interrogation.
NORRIS	It is not. It's conversation.
BONNIE	He's a famous author.
NORRIS	He is not. He's a reporter.
BONNIE	Well. His name is always in the paper.

Beat.

NICK	Why don't we just sip brandy.
NORRIS	I'm not having any.
NICK	Have some.
NORRIS	I don't want any.
NICK	That's not my fault, is it?
NORRIS	Why won't you answer my question?
NICK	Why don't you answer mine?
NORRIS	What question?
NICK	Where's Kevin?
BONNIE	Nick!
NICK	Sorry.
NORRIS	You don't have to apologize. Just shut up.
NICK	Fine. End of conversation.
NORRIS	We did not have a conversation!

NICK   My lips are sealed. (*drinking*)

                Short pause.

NORRIS   I haven't seen Guy in ages. I mean since that
                party at the Gibson's. He had too much to drink
                and threw up in the jacuzzi.

                Silence.

NORRIS   I put him in the shower.

NICK   Thank you so much.

NORRIS   Well you were away. Again.

NICK   So?

NORRIS   He said he blacked out. I didn't think people
                really did black out, except in movies. But I
                think he did. Do you think he really can't
                remember?

NICK   I can't imagine why he'd want to remember
                throwing up in the Gibson's jacuzzi.

BONNIE   Who are the Gibson's?

NORRIS   Friends of Nick's. I sold them their computer.

NICK   Bob and Samantha.

NORRIS   I thought he was supposed to be here for dinner.

BONNIE   I don't know Bob Gibson. Why would I invite
                him for dinner?

NORRIS   Guy!

BONNIE   Oh.

NORRIS   Where is he?

BONNIE   He's working.

NORRIS   At this hour?

BONNIE   That's what Nick told me.

NORRIS   Oh.

NICK   Oh, what?

NORRIS   Oh, he's working late, that's all.

NICK   I assume that means something very different in your household. In mine it means he's working late.

Pause.

NORRIS   Why is it that when my friends irritate me, they don't irritate me, and when my family does, they do?

BONNIE   That's a loaded question, Norris.

NICK   I think it was rhetorical.

NORRIS   I don't expect you to answer it.

BONNIE   That's what he meant.

NORRIS   Why didn't he say so?

BONNIE *smiles at* NICK. NORRIS *notices but does not say anything.* *Pause.*

GLEN   I thought we were having a conversation.

NICK   We were.

NORRIS	We were trying to have a conversation. Or at least I was. But no one else seems to want to, so I will just shut up.
NICK	Fine.
	Silence.
NORRIS	This is stupid.
	Silence.
NORRIS	It is.
	Silence.
NORRIS	Oh alright. It took us three hours to get up here today, not including the half hour at McDonald's when the boys locked all the bathroom stalls and Kevin had to crawl under and open them.
NICK	Why'd he "have to" do that?
GLEN	He probably had to go to the bathroom.
BONNIE	We've dropped that subject. Kevin, I mean.
	Pause.
NORRIS	You all pick on me. You do, you know. Do you realize that? (*beat*) You always have something to say about the way I live my life. You always talk about Kevin behind his back, and you always talk about me behind my back, to my face. And I'm sick and tired of you telling me to spank my children. I don't spank my children. If you've got a problem with the twins, just tell them. They're intelligent human beings. Talk to them. Because nobody spanks my children but me! (*beat*) And I don't spank them.
NICK	Is there any pie left?

NORRIS   How can you possibly eat any more? Didn't you
                get enough at dinner? It certainly looked as if you
                did.

BONNIE   There's the piece you were saving for Guy. In the
                fridge.

NICK   Thank you.

                      NICK *exits to the kitchen.*

GLEN   (*cheerfully*) I'll have a conversation.

BONNIE   I will too.

NORRIS   You're both reading. You're not even listening to
                me.

                      GLEN *puts down his paper.* BONNIE
                      stacks the travel brochures.

GLEN   What do you want to talk about?

                      NICK *re-enters from kitchen.*

NICK   Is Kevin wearing my coat?

NORRIS   (*pointedly*) I don't want to talk anymore.

BONNIE   Norris, don't be like that. Nick, shut up.

NORRIS   Like what?

NICK   What did I say?

BONNIE   Don't talk about Kevin.

NICK   But...

BONNIE   Enough.

GLEN   How are the kids, Norris?

NORRIS   Didn't you see them at dinner?

BONNIE   He means "How are they?"

NORRIS   They're fine!

GLEN   How's the first grade?

NORRIS   They're in the second.

BONNIE   But do they like it?

NORRIS   No.

GLEN   Are they getting good grades?

NORRIS   So. so.

BONNIE   And you?

NORRIS   Me?

BONNIE   How are you doing?

NORRIS   O.K.

BONNIE   Is something wrong? You know, Kevin was
                quiet, but you've been talking too much.

NORRIS   Thank you.

GLEN   Is that what this is all about?

BONNIE   Glen.

NORRIS   Is that what what is all about?

GLEN   You.

NORRIS   What about me?

BONNIE   What's wrong?

NORRIS   Nothing is wrong. Absolutely nothing.

BONNIE   Nothing?

NORRIS   I said nothing, didn't I? Nothing.Everything is fine. Nothing that a few thousand bucks wouldn't fix. Or some new Reeboks for the boys.

                    KEVIN *enters and everyone looks at him.*

KEVIN   I just saw a skunk go into your garage.

NICK   He *is* wearing my coat.

BONNIE   (*to* Kevin) Are you sure?

NICK   That's the coat I arrived in.

GLEN   A skunk?

NORRIS   Takes one to know one.

KEVIN   Don't start.

BONNIE   Are you sure it wasn't a cat?

GLEN   The Seligman's have a marmalade tabby.

KEVIN   It was a black thing, about so big, with a white stripe down its back.

BONNIE   What could it be?

KEVIN   A skunk!

NICK   It didn't spray you, did it?

BONNIE   We'd smell him if it did.

NORRIS	I can smell him from here.
GLEN	I don't smell anything.
NICK	Can I have my coat back?
BONNIE	Are you going out?
GLEN	I hope the windows are up in the car.
NICK	No, I just want my coat back.
NORRIS	Why are you wearing Nick's coat?
NICK	It's no big deal, Norris.
KEVIN	It was by the door.
BONNIE	(*to* Glen) Hadn't someone better check?
GLEN	How am I going to check? I'll get sprayed.
BONNIE	Not you. You can't go out in this weather. Kevin, will you check?
NICK	Not in my coat!
NORRIS	Give Nick his coat back.
BONNIE	I don't want a skunk in my car.
GLEN	I'm sure I put the windows up.
BONNIE	You're just saying that.
KEVIN	(*to* Nick) Here. (*handing him the coat*)
BONNIE	Nick, you check.
NICK	Dad said he put the windows up.
BONNIE	He's not really sure, though.

GLEN   I never said I put the windows down! I only
                wondered if they were up.

BONNIE   I'll check.

GLEN   Don't be silly. You can't go out there in the dark.
                You'll trip over something.

BONNIE   Nick, let me have your coat.

NORRIS   I'll go.

GLEN   (to BONNIE) You're not going out there.

NORRIS   I said I'll go. Give me your coat (reaching for the
                coat).

NICK   Doesn't anyone else have a coat in this house?

NORRIS   You're so selfish.

NICK   Selfish? I don't want my coat to get sprayed by a
                skunk. O.K?

GLEN   I'll go.

BONNIE   You'll catch your death.

GLEN   I'm going to check the windows.

NORRIS   (to Kevin) Now see what you've done?

KEVIN   What've I done?

NORRIS   You've started a fight.

KEVIN   Nobody's fighting in here.

GLEN   Where's the flashlight?

BONNIE   The batteries are dead.

GLEN   I put them on your shopping list.

BONNIE	I forgot them.
GLEN	Damn it, Bonnie. That's twice now.
NORRIS	(*to* Kevin) See?
BONNIE	Damn it yourself, you old fart. If you want batteries, you buy batteries.

BONNIE *exits.*

GLEN	Don't go out there! Bonnie, come back here.

GLEN *exits.*

NICK	(*to* NORRIS) Well?
NORRIS	Well what?
NICK	I thought you were going too.
NORRIS	I am.

NORRIS *exits.* NICK *and* KEVIN *eye each other.* NICK *puts his coat on a chair.*

NICK	Is it cold out there?
KEVIN	Getting there.
NICK	Would you like a drink to warm you up?
KEVIN	Any beer left?
NICK	How about a brandy?
KEVIN	(*shrugging*) If that's all there is.
NICK	'Fraid so. Till the champagne, anyway. (*going for drink*) So, you and Norris had a big fight.

KEVIN   She told you?

NICK   You know Norris.

KEVIN   She said she wouldn't. She made me swear I
                   wouldn't bring it up. She said that she couldn't
                   possibly face any of you, but I guess she just
                   said that 'cause she wanted to bring it up first and
                   prejudice you all against me...if that's possible
                   under the circumstances...which I suppose it is,
                   given the way your dad feels about me and the
                   way Norris can make even the twins feel guilty.

NICK   Yeah. Well. You know Norris.

KEVIN   Did she tell you what it was about?

NICK   Not in so many words.

KEVIN   God damn it. She did, didn't she? Of course she
                   did, because she said she wouldn't.

NICK   Well...

KEVIN   Damn her!

NICK   Calm down. (*handing him drink*) She didn't say
                   anything...

KEVIN   I should have known she would tell all of you
                   before I could get out. She wants me to feel
                   worse that I already do.

NICK   Get out?

KEVIN   I think it's best, don't you? I mean, wouldn't you
                   want to?

NICK   Hey, Kevin, look, honestly...

KEVIN   What do you think?

NICK   Me?

KEVIN	What do you think?
NICK	Well, it's really none of my business...
KEVIN	You're family. I mean, I know you're her family first, but you're still my family still.
NICK	I know, but...I don't want to interfere.
KEVIN	No. Really. I want your opinion.
NICK	You do?
KEVIN	Sure I do.
NICK	I'm flattered.
KEVIN	Well?
NICK	Well...
KEVIN	Look, don't be embarrassed. I'm not embarrassed. And hell, I'm the one who should be embarrassed, if anybody is going to be...And Norris should be too, of course, except she's not because she's, well, she's Norris.
NICK	I'm not embarrassed Kevin, it's just that...well...I don't know what to say.
KEVIN	I want your opinion.
NICK	Oh shit Kevin, I'm sorry...
KEVIN	Thanks.
NICK	Thanks?
KEVIN	I'm...sort of glad you're on my side.
NICK	Me? I'm not on anyone's side.

KEVIN   You know, even beside the point, I really do hate babies.

NICK   Babies?

KEVIN   Don't you?

NICK   Well, I...

KEVIN   I can't stand 'em. I mean, these guys are great and all, even though they've got this thing now about locking me out of the toilet. But that's O.K. I mean, the pediatrician says it's O.K. because it's part of their hang up with me being their dad and their wanting to be, like, artists. But they're not babies anymore. Thank God. I mean, I hate babies, don't you?

NICK   Well...yeah.

KEVIN   (*smiling*) Yeah?

NICK   Well, let's face it. I mean, I know you've had some and all...but they're boring, aren't they?

KEVIN   Boring?

NICK   Oh, I know they can't help it. Don't get me wrong. They don't know any better. But, I mean, it's the ripple effect that bothers me. And I don't mean grown men goo-gooing over a cradle — that's brief and relatively painless. It's like gas, actually.

KEVIN   You mean colic?

NICK   Pardon?

KEVIN   Colic.

NICK   Well...um...no, Kevin. What I really mean, is
                the way babies deaden whole circles of people.
                You know? Otherwise articulate adults suddenly
                say they're going to the potty, and insist that you
                applaud their offspring if it makes number two...

KEVIN   (*proud*) The boys call it a B.M. now.

NICK   No kidding?

KEVIN   The pediatrician thinks its best.

NICK   Well, he'd know, wouldn't he?

KEVIN   (*explaining*) Bowel Movement.

NICK   Right. I know.

KEVIN   Sorry, did I cut you off just then?

NICK   No, I was...I was...Never mind.

KEVIN   (*worried*) The twins are O.K. though, aren't'
                they?

NICK   Oh. Yeah. (*beat*) They're great, Kevin.

KEVIN   It's just babies.

NICK   Right. Just babies.

KEVIN   They're so ugly.

NICK   Boring and ugly.

KEVIN   Right. Well, ugly.

                NORRIS *enters.*

NORRIS   It's freezing out there.

KEVIN   Why didn't you wear a coat?

NORRIS   (*glance*) I see you're into the brandy.

KEVIN   They're out of beer.

NICK   Did you see a skunk?

NORRIS   Do I smell like I saw a skunk?

NICK   No. But you sound like you did.

NORRIS   Is that a joke?

KEVIN   (*suddenly*) Nick agrees with me.

NICK   What?

KEVIN   He said he did.

NICK   Kevin, I...

NORRIS   He doesn't even know what you're talking about.

KEVIN   He does too.

NORRIS   How would he know, unless you told him? And you swore that you absolutely would not bring it up in this house!

KEVIN   Me!? You're the one who told him everything.

NORRIS   I did not.

KEVIN   Nick, tell her.

NICK   Tell her what?

NORRIS   What you told me.

NICK   What did I tell you?

KEVIN   You know.

NICK   About babies?

NORRIS	Babies!
KEVIN	Go on.
NORRIS	(*to* KEVIN) You did tell him! You bastard!
KEVIN	You bitch!
NORRIS	Don't call me that word!
KEVIN	Bitch!
NORRIS	Bastard!
NICK	I'm going to see how mom and dad are doing with the skunk.
NORRIS	Don't you dare tell them!
NICK	Believe me, I won't.
KEVIN	You're going to wake up the twins with your screeching.
NORRIS	What does Nick know about babies, anyhow?
NICK	Leave me out of this. Whatever it is.
KEVIN	Come on Nick, don't chicken out now.
NORRIS	(*to* NICK) Don't interfere!
NICK	Jesus, you two. All I want to do is get out of your line of fire.
KEVIN	Hell Nick, you started it.
NICK	Started what?
NORRIS	What did he start?
KEVIN	Tell her.

NICK   Tell her what?

NORRIS   Tell me what?

KEVIN   What you said.

NICK   What did I say?

NORRIS   What did you say?

NICK   I don't know!

KEVIN   Norris, that's it. Your family is cracked. (*to*
                  NICK) A minute ago you were all on my side
                  "buddy-buddy-have-another-beer-and-slap-on-the-
                  backside" What happened, Nick? Hunh? What
                  happened? Family first?

NORRIS   Oh, sure. Out it comes. Have another brandy
                  Kevin. And when you run out of brandy maybe
                  you can switch to anti-freeze. I'm sure I saw
                  some out in the garage.

                            KEVIN *pointedly puts down his glass
                            and folds his arms.*

KEVIN   Satisfied?

                            Pause.

NICK   You want another?

KEVIN   No I don't want another. But if I did want another
                  I would have another. And another.

NICK   But you don't?

NORRIS   No he doesn't.

KEVIN   (*to* NORRIS) I said I didn't! (*to* NICK) But if I
                  did I would!

BONNIE *and* GLEN *enter laughing.*

NORRIS   What's so funny?

BONNIE   The Seligman's cat got sprayed.

NORRIS   That's horrible.

BONNIE   No it's not. That animal is always putting paw prints on the hood of the car.

NORRIS   Is it O.K.?

BONNIE   It stinks.

NORRIS   Poor thing.

BONNIE   Glen shooed it home.

NORRIS   Did you warn the Seligman's?

BONNIE   There's no need.

GLEN   They've got a cat door.

NICK, GLEN *and* BONNIE *laugh.*

KEVIN   I rest my case.

KEVIN *starts to exit.*

NORRIS   Where are you going?

GLEN   What case?

NICK   Us.

GLEN   What about us?

BONNIE   Don't go outside. It stinks out there.

KEVIN   (*looking at* NORRIS) It stinks in here.

                        KEVIN *exits.*

NORRIS   Where are you going?!

                        KEVIN *does not answer.*

GLEN   What case? Norris?

NICK   He thinks we're cracked.

NORRIS   You are!

BONNIE   Is that what you were arguing about?

NORRIS   No mother. Because on that case, there is nothing to argue about.

GLEN   He's got a lot of nerve, for a wedding photographer.

NICK   He hates babies.

BONNIE   What? Don't be silly.

NICK   He thinks they're ugly.

BONNIE   Why are you saying that?

NORRIS   Is that what he said to you?

NICK   He said that he can't stand 'em.

BONNIE   He didn't. I can't believe it.

GLEN   I can.

BONNIE   He said that about his own children?

NICK   No...

BONNIE   I didn't think so.

NICK	He said it about babies. Generic babies.
BONNIE	Oh, well then.
NORRIS	Oh well then, what? Is that supposed to mean that it's O.K.? Now you're going to defend him I suppose, just because I'm not.
BONNIE	No, Norris. It means that I can understand that. It makes perfect sense to me.
GLEN	Me too.
NORRIS	What?
BONNIE	I don't like babies.
NORRIS	I don't want to hear this.
BONNIE	Did you think a third baby in this family just "didn't happen"? I got tired of being a parent. Haven't you?
NORRIS	Stop it.
BONNIE	And I don't think it's uncommon either.
NORRIS	I'll never be like that.
BONNIE	Possibly.
NORRIS	Never.
BONNIE	I don't mean that one morning I thought I'd push your pram into traffic, honey. Or that I thought I'd throw you out on the street when you screamed at me, or broke something, or stuck a butter knife into the insulation of the freezer when you tried to defrost it for me.
NORRIS	That was twenty-three years ago!

BONNIE	Look, I know you think I'm a bad mother, that way...
NORRIS	(*too quickly*) I do not.
BONNIE	That way.
NORRIS	(pause) What way?
BONNIE	Babysitting the children. Grandchildren. Making cakes. In fact, I was never so glad as when I could go out without having to find a sitter for you and Nicky.
NORRIS	You hate me.
BONNIE	I do not.
NORRIS	You hate my children.
BONNIE	I do not.
NORRIS	You hate your grandchildren!
BONNIE	I do not.
NORRIS	You're so incredibly selfish!
BONNIE	Maybe.

NORRIS *is taken aback*

BONNIE	Maybe I am. But I do not hate you. Or your children. Or my grandchildren. O.K.?
GLEN	O.K.

Pause.

NICK	(*beat*) Oh.

NORRIS	(*irritated*) Oh what?
NICK	You're going to have another, aren't you?
GLEN	Another?
BONNIE	Is that it?
NICK	And he doesn't want you to?
GLEN	Another?
BONNIE	(*innocently*) I thought Kevin had a vasectomy.
NORRIS	Mother!
BONNIE	Am I wrong?
GLEN	Another baby?
BONNIE	Oh...

There is a sound in the hall.

NORRIS	What are you doing out there?
KEVIN	(*off*) Nothing.
NORRIS	Why are you making so much noise?
KEVIN	(off) I'm not.
NORRIS	Why have you got the front door open?
KEVIN	(*off*) I don't.

The front door slams. Beat.

NORRIS	I suppose you're all going to be shocked now.

GLEN   Why should we be shocked? You're having another baby. What's to be shocked about that? You are a little old. Is that it? Or don't you want it?

NICK   Something like that.

BONNIE   Kevin isn't the father.

NORRIS   I didn't say that!

GLEN   Who is?

BONNIE   Glen.

GLEN   What?

BONNIE   What kind of a question is that?

NORRIS   Are you scandalized?

GLEN   I don't know yet. Who's the father?

NICK   How far along are you?

NORRIS   What difference does it make?

GLEN   Do you know who the father is?

NORRIS   Of course I think I know who the father is.

GLEN   Good.

BONNIE   Is "who?" a reasonable question?

NORRIS   Please! I had no intention of discussing this with any of you. It is none of your business. I wish we'd never come up here for this stupid dinner. This is between Kevin and me and...(*stopping herself*).

                        Pause.

GLEN   You and whom?

NICK   (*quickly*) Don't say Greg Wallace. He is such an asshole.

GLEN   Who's he?

BONNIE   Kevin's partner.

NORRIS   No it is not Greg Wallace! Damn it, I'm getting out of here.

BONNIE   Where are you going?

NORRIS   Out.

GLEN   Look out for the skunk.

NORRIS   Oh fuck the skunk.

> NORRIS *grabs* NICK's *coat and runs out.*

NICK   Hey! She took my coat.

BONNIE   It's cold.

> *Pause.*

GLEN   Well.

BONNIE   Well what?

GLEN   Well, well.

BONNIE   Don't do your old man act.

GLEN   I am an old man.

BONNIE   Pooh.

GLEN   And you're an old woman.

BONNIE	Double pooh.
NICK	Should I go after her?
BONNIE	What are you going to say if you do?
NICK	I don't know.
GLEN	You didn't run after Kevin.
NICK	He didn't want me to.
BONNIE	You think she does?
NICK	Probably not.
BONNIE	I suppose you could run after her if you wanted to, but it's so cold and smelly out there that I don't think she'll be long. And she does have your coat, after all, so you wouldn't last more than a few minutes; so if she does want to talk you'd be better off waiting until she comes back in.

KEVIN *enters wearing a hat and coat.*

BONNIE	Oh, hello Kevin. You're awfully bundled up.
KEVIN	Where's Norris?
GLEN	Out.
KEVIN	Out where?
BONNIE	She ran out the back door when you went out the front.
NICK	In my coat.
KEVIN	Tell her I'm taking the twins to the city.
BONNIE	Why are you doing that?

KEVIN	We're going to my mother's house.
BONNIE	This is sudden. Where are the boys?
KEVIN	In the car.
GLEN	Your car's got a flat.
KEVIN	What?
GLEN	The right rear tire looks low.
KEVIN	Shit.
BONNIE	How do you know?
GLEN	The Seligman's cat was under his car.
KEVIN	Have you got a pump?
BONNIE	You can't go, Kevin. I bought champagne.
GLEN	He wants to go, Bonnie.
NICK	(*quickly*) Do you need any help?
KEVIN	Help?
NICK	I mean, with the kids. Loading the car.
KEVIN	It's loaded. I carried them down in the bedspread.
BONNIE	My grandmother knitted that bedspread.
KEVIN	I'll bring it back.
BONNIE	That's O.K. Keep it. Norris always wanted it anyway. Now it's hers.
GLEN	He doesn't need a blanket. He needs a pump.
BONNIE	Shouldn't you wait for Norris?

GLEN   He can pump up a tire on his own at least, can't
              he?

                        A car is heard.

BONNIE   Now who's that?

KEVIN   Damn her. It's Norris I bet.

GLEN   She won't get very far.

KEVIN   She's stolen my car!

                        KEVIN *runs out.*

NICK   She's got my coat!

                        NICK *exits.*

GLEN   You know, Bonnie, we have lived beyond the age
              of scandal.

BONNIE   What are you talking about?

GLEN   We have even lived long enough to live beyond
              the very recent age when being caught was
              considered the crime.

BONNIE   We're not that old.

GLEN   We live, my darling, in an age when scandal has
              been elevated to the routine.

BONNIE   What scandal?

GLEN   And it's not that it doesn't matter, which would
              be simple cynicism— it's that it does matter in a
              positive way, as a credential even, that makes it
              all so "new."

BONNIE   There's nothing new about being pregnant.

GLEN   The morality which once upon a time informed
        our behaviour, has become, for all intents and
        purposes, the amorality, which is modern
        morality.

BONNIE You can be very pompous.

GLEN   It's the fate, my darling, of dying lawyers.

                NICK *re-enters, followed by* KEVIN.

NICK   She's gone.

GLEN   Gone where?

NICK   She drove off.

GLEN   Not in my car, I hope.

KEVIN   In my car.

BONNIE I thought the tire was flat.

GLEN   I said it was low.

KEVIN   She's too stupid to notice.

BONNIE Oh dear. I hope she knows she's got the boys
        with her. I mean, I hope she isn't planning on
        going somewhere and...parking the car.

GLEN   Where would she go?

BONNIE To *him*, silly.

GLEN   Him who?

KEVIN   Yeah. Him who?

BONNIE You know. (*beat*) Don't you?

KEVIN   (*bluffing*) Of course I know.

NICK	You want to go after her?
GLEN	In whose car?
NICK	My car!
GLEN	Go ahead.
KEVIN	(*to* NICK) Really?
GLEN	Be my guest.
NICK	Go ahead. I'll just get my keys...
BONNIE	What's the matter?
NICK	They're in my coat pocket.

GLEN *picks up the paper.*

BONNIE	Oh no.
NICK	And my wallet.
BONNIE	Well she won't steal anything.
KEVIN	I wouldn't be so sure.
BONNIE	She is your sister after all.
NICK	I don't believe this.
BONNIE	Glen. (*beat*) Glen!
GLEN	What?
BONNIE	Hand over the keys.
GLEN	What keys?
BONNIE	To the car.

GLEN	No.
BONNIE	Where are they?
GLEN	Where are what?
BONNIE	Never mind Kevin. My set is hanging by the kitchen door. Take it.
KEVIN	Thanks, Mrs. Beacham.
BONNIE	You'd better hurry. She drives too fast, you know.
KEVIN	I know.
BONNIE	Run along.
KEVIN	Thanks.
NICK	Sorry about the...(*stopping himself*)
GLEN	The what?

KEVIN *exits.*

BONNIE	The baby, I suppose you were going to say. But there's not much point in feeling sorry about that. It. Whatever. Is there? I think you'd be safe feeling sorry *for* it, however, since it's sort of being lobbed over the fence, isn't it?
GLEN	Who is the father, do you think?
NICK	She didn't say it wasn't Kevin.
BONNIE	No, but I don't think that was necessary, do you? If it was Kevin, she would have said so. Even if there was a remote possibility that it could have been Kevin, she would have said so. And there is a remote possibility, you know.

BONNIE   (*continued*) Vasectomies can be reversed every
                  once in a blue moon. But since she didn't even
                  bother to grasp at that straw, it's more than
                  likely that she feels guilty about whoever the
                  father really is.

GLEN   What do we do?

BONNIE   Do we have to do anything?

GLEN   She's still our daughter.

BONNIE   We could worry, I suppose. Lose some sleep.
                  And pretend that we're not any more confused
                  than she is. That's what's expected.

NICK   Mom, I'm surprised...

BONNIE   By me?

NICK   You're awfully calm.

BONNIE   It's the brandy, I suppose.

GLEN   She's pretending.

BONNIE   What?

GLEN   See?

NICK   See what?

GLEN   She's pretending.

NICK   Are you pretending, mom?

BONNIE   No.

GLEN   See?

NICK   Is that pretending?

BONNIE	Norris is middle-aged, and has been selling typewriters for seventeen years.
GLEN	So?
BONNIE	Having babies is more like a hobby than a talent.
GLEN	Is that any way to talk to your own son?
BONNIE	(*to* NICK) Are you shocked?
NICK	Um. No.
BONNIE	Do you know what death does?
GLEN	Bonnie, wait.
NICK	Whose death?
BONNIE	Just death. Big death. Death on a horse. Death with a scythe...try saying that quickly...death with a scythe.
GLEN	Should I get the champagne?
NICK	Death with a scythe.
BONNIE	It makes it very easy to accept anything in the world. — except death, of course. Death is not easy to accept, despite appearances. It's just that once you have got your head around it, the world never really comes back into focus. At least not the way it was. (*smiling*) Is that New Age thought?
GLEN	No, it's just plain old age.
BONNIE	It's such an ooga booga word. It's such an ooga booga subject, really. Dr. Meissner was very funny about it. He said it was like when someone farts in public, at a formal dinner was the example he gave, and nobody really knows

BONNIE	(*continued*) each other well, and they all have to pretend that it's roses. Or that it's not there at all.
NICK	Is that the Dr. Meissner I know?
GLEN	Rob.
NICK	He gave Norris and me all our allergy shots. He was the one that the needle broke when it was in my arm and he just laughed. Is he still practicing?
BONNIE	No dear, he's dead.
NICK	I didn't know that.
BONNIE	I'm sure I told you. He killed himself about a month ago. Didn't I send you the clipping?
NICK	...no.
BONNIE	Over in Victoria Park. On a bench. He had a cuban cigar in his pocket. *The New York Times* crossword in his lap. And a flask of Chivas Regal. It was perfect really. Or it would have been if a child hadn't found him. Poor thing. His bowels had "relaxed" apparently. One of us should have found him, you know Glen. Your dad or I wouldn't have minded. But he didn't think that part through, or I'm sure he would have left us a note, or something. Telling us where.
NICK	Why did he kill himself?

BONNIE *smiles at* GLEN.

NICK	Did he tell you?
GLEN	Well, Nick. I know you don't know much about baseball, but it's the best line I can come up with. It was over before it was over.

BONNIE	You don't know anything about baseball either.
NICK	He was sick?
BONNIE	Euphemistically.
GLEN	Should I get the champagne?
BONNIE	Shouldn't we wait for Norris?
GLEN	We don't know if she's coming back.
BONNIE	That's true.
NICK	She'd better be. She's got my coat.
BONNIE	You can borrow one of Glen's. Actually, you can have one of Glen's.
NICK	I like my coat.
BONNIE	Nick...
NICK	It cost a lot of money.
BONNIE	Ssshh.
NICK	What?
BONNIE	Nick...
NICK	Yes?
BONNIE	You've been spared a lot.
NICK	What?
BONNIE	We all have. This family. But then, we're middle class, aren't we? We aren't really affected by things, except taxes. We can vote anyone into office...the country could fall apart...and it doesn't make any real difference — except taxes. There is no way around it.

BONNIE   (*continued*) I've thought this all through. I'm not foaming at the mouth, and I may not know what I'm talking about, but I have certainly thought it through.

We are the middle class. You, Norris, me, Glen, Kevin, the twins. All of us. Sure, I know you drive an expensive car now, and Kevin's got all the right camera equipment and we've travelled a lot and consider it normal. We even consider ourselves normal — which is always presumptuous, no matter what class you come from. But we're safe, you know?

Oh, I know there was a burglary at the Cole's two doors down, and Betty Tyler was mugged in the K Mart parking lot — or she says she was — and Doug Blake shot Moira over their divorce settlement...and I know you're homosexual, and you know that that's just fine with us — now — and you also know that it wasn't at first, when you were still pretending that you couldn't make up your mind and told us lies about where you were and who answered your phone and...well...and all that. But you're a middle-class homosexual, which means you're middle-class first, and then a homosexual. Gay, sorry. Gay.

And by that I don't mean that you have a Cuisinart and eat raddiccio — I mean you're still protected, because your middle classness makes it O.K. Our middle-classness makes it O.K. Because the middle class is normal. So everything you do is normal. Of course there's AIDS, which we also don't talk about because we're middle class. Because we don't want to talk about it because we don't have to and pray to God we never will without actually praying.
But there's also Guy, and you seem happy and I think you are — I hope you are. And you trust him, so we have no choice but to trust him too, which is also very middle class of us.
What else can we do?

BONNIE	(*continued*) And Norris too. The twins, the husband, the dishwasher, the Reeboks she makes us buy for the twins. And now this third baby on the way too, whoever the father is. Because whoever the father is, this baby is going to be safe. If she doesn't have a...miscarriage...or whatever.

Pause.

GLEN	Champagne?
BONNIE	Do you know what we're going to ask you to accept as normal now? Without flinching?
NICK	...No...
GLEN	Norris too.
NICK	What?
BONNIE	Death.
NICK	What?
BONNIE	Glen wants to die.
GLEN	Like Dr. Meissner.
NICK	What?
BONNIE	It's your turn.
NICK	Are you serious?

GLEN *smiles.*

BONNIE	And don't get moral with us. You haven't got a foot to stand on.
GLEN	Leg.

NICK	I don't understand...
GLEN	Leg to stand on. Not foot.

NORRIS *rushes into the room.*

NORRIS	Call the police.
BONNIE	Norris, what are you doing back here? Where's Kevin?
NORRIS	Call the police.
BONNIE	What for? Where are the twins? Have you had an accident?
NORRIS	Kevin kidnapped my children.
GLEN	How?
NORRIS	What do you mean how? He took them.
GLEN	I thought they were in the car with you.
BONNIE	They were.
NORRIS	How did you know that?
BONNIE	Kevin told us.
NORRIS	You mean you didn't stop him?
GLEN	You drove off in Kevin's car.
NORRIS	*My* car!
GLEN	Then how can Kevin have the twins? And how can you be here?
NORRIS	(*irritated*) I only got a couple of blocks.
BONNIE	(*to* GLEN) Kevin caught up with her.

NORRIS	I got a flat.
GLEN	I thought it looked low.
NORRIS	Then why didn't you say so!
GLEN	I did.
BONNIE	Is Kevin changing the tire for you?
NORRIS	No! He drove right past me! In your car!
BONNIE	That wasn't very nice...
NORRIS	He grabbed the boys.
BONNIE	What do you mean he grabbed them?
NORRIS	He grabbed them.
BONNIE	I thought they were in your car.
GLEN	They were.
BONNIE	You mean you left them in the car while you walked back here? That wasn't very safe.
NORRIS	By the time I got back to my car, Kevin had already loaded them into your car and kidnapped them.
NICK	He didn't kidnap them! He's taking them to his mother's house.
NORRIS	What?
BONNIE	That's what he told us.
NORRIS	Then why didn't you tell me?!
GLEN	You crept out the back door, Norry.
NORRIS	I did not "creep out."

NICK	For God's sake, Norris! Shut up!
BONNIE	Please don't fight.
NICK	We're not fighting!
NORRIS	My children have been taken!
BONNIE	Don't exaggerate either.
NORRIS	Exaggerate!?
BONNIE	You know they're perfectly safe.
GLEN	At least they're not sitting in a car by the side of the road.
BONNIE	Glen.
NORRIS	I'm calling the police.
NICK	Don't do that.
NORRIS	Don't tell me what to do.
BONNIE	Don't call the police. There's no point.
NORRIS	Don't you tell me what to do either.
GLEN	Norris, don't.
NORRIS	(*beat*) Why can't I call the police? My children have been kidnapped.
BONNIE	If you send the police to your poor old mother-in-law's and they find the twins in their beds, with grandmother Spanner sitting in a rocking chair beside them, what are you going to say?

Pause.

NICK	Dad wants to kill himself.

NORRIS   What?

GLEN   I do not.

NICK   (*glaring at* GLEN) Then what the hell did you
                tell me all that for?

NORRIS   All what?

BONNIE   He wants to *die*.

NORRIS   What?

BONNIE   (*to* NORRIS) He doesn't want to kill himself.

NICK   What?

BONNIE   He never said he wanted to kill himself. He just
                thinks it's morally superior.

GLEN   Given the choice, I would rather be killed.

                Beat. GLEN *starts to exit.*
                Black out.

Act Two

A short time later. NICK *drinks,* NORRIS *paces, and* BONNIE *reads.*

NORRIS   I'm going to call Dr. Meissner.

BONNIE   Don't be ridiculous.

NICK   She wasn't here.

BONNIE   Oh, right.

NORRIS   He'll talk some sense into you.

NICK   Norris...

NORRIS   He'll be appalled.

BONNIE   Norris...

NORRIS   I mean how sick can Daddy be? He doesn't look that sick. What does Dr. Meissner say? I thought remission meant a person was getting better.

NICK   Norris...

NORRIS   What about that stuff they make out of apricots? I remember reading about it at the check out. Steve McQueen took it. What's it called?

BONNIE	Laetrile.
NORRIS	That's it. What does Dr. Meissner say? Surely he can get some for us. Christ, daddy can go to Mexico.
BONNIE	He's not interested in a vacation, Norris.
NORRIS	To a clinic!
NICK	Norris...
NORRIS	You can get laetrile in Mexico.
BONNIE	Norris, we've been where you are.
NORRIS	Well you should be in Mexico.
NICK	It doesn't work, Norris.
NORRIS	How do you know?
NICK	It's quackery.
NORRIS	You take vitamins, don't you?
NICK	That doesn't matter. I'm healthy.
NORRIS	Because you take vitamins.
NICK	Vitamins only help me because I'm healthy.
NORRIS	God, you're insensitive Nick.
NICK	Oh, I'm sorry Norris. Is this your personal crisis? I'm afraid, in fact, you're going to have to share this one.
NORRIS	You know what I hate most about you Nick?

NICK   No, Norris, I don't. And what a perfect time for you to tell me, don't you think? God forbid that the focus of any conversation should go off you for two minutes.

NORRIS   That's what I hate about you. Right there. The way you talk when you should be upset and you're not.You know, you just sail through arguments without putting up a fight.

BONNIE   We're not arguing.

NORRIS   You're so — calm, Nick! How can you just watch your father kill himself?

BONNIE   Norris, he's just getting champagne.

NICK   And I am just trying to listen, as calmly as possible, to what he's saying.

NORRIS   Oh, I see. You approve, do you?

NICK   I didn't say that.

NORRIS   I bet you can't wait to get your hands on his stamp collection.

BONNIE   Norris!

NICK   (*biting his lip*) I said I am trying to stay calm.

NORRIS   You don't look like you have to try, Nick. And I have to ask myself why.

NICK   Well, I can hear the calculator running in your head.

BONNIE   Nick!

NICK   Sorry.

NORRIS   I love my father!

NICK   I love my father!

NORRIS	I love him more than you do!
NICK	Oh, Christ.

Pause.

NORRIS	Now he's calm again. Just like that.
NICK	Norris, my hand is shaking right here. And it's shaking for two reasons. It's shaking because I want to slug you and it's shaking because I know better than to slug you.

(*to* BONNIE) Maybe this is only one aspect of my middle class neurosis,

(*to* NORRIS) but it is one that you should not take for granted as you go through life telling people what to do. And you should also know that my hand is not going to stop shaking when I stop wanting to hit you.

And that has nothing to do with you! That has to do with my middle-class mortgage and my expensive car payments and my job at the paper and the price of radiccio and Guy and the number of brandies I've had after dinner. And Dad, too, for Christ's sake! O.K.?

Just because I'm being reasonable does not mean I'm reasonable. O.K.?

Beat.

NORRIS	O.K. what? You didn't say anything.
BONNIE	He has a reasonable urge to hit you Norris, but he's not going to do it.
NORRIS	(*to* NICK) Is that a threat? Or a surrender?
BONNIE	Both.

NORRIS	Well I don't care. I only tell people what to do because I know what they should do.(*after a beat, to* BONNIE, *with forced calm*) What's Dr. Meissner's number?
BONNIE	His number?
NORRIS	When did daddy last see him?
BONNIE	About a month ago. Norris...
NORRIS	A month ago?
NICK	At his funeral.
NORRIS	What?
BONNIE	He killed himself, darling.

NORRIS *is stunned.*

BONNIE	It was quite lovely, really. If that sort of thing can be lovely. Or maybe lovely *is* the wrong word....He was ready, that's all. He and your father used to compare x-rays. Rob's number was up first. At least that's how he described it in layman's terms. His was in the brain, of course, and so he didn't really have much choice...about when, I mean. The headaches were continual. Pain's the worst part. That's what your father says.

There is a loud bang in the kitchen.

NORRIS	What was that?
BONNIE	A bang.
NORRIS	Oh God, what's he done?
NICK	Dad?

NORRIS	He hasn't shot himself, has he?
BONNIE	It's just a bang.
NORRIS	Daddy?
BONNIE	It's the champagne cork, Norris.
NICK	Is this why you bought champagne?
BONNIE	Your father thinks that euthanasia is the epitome of decadence.
NORRIS	That's sick.

GLEN *enters with a tray of champagne.*

GLEN	Here we are.
NORRIS	Daddy, I cannot allow you to do this.
GLEN	Do what?
BONNIE	It's only champagne.
NORRIS	(*firmly*) You need — counselling. I mean, aren't they supposed to do that when there's a serious illness? I'm sure they are. They always do in every serious illness movie I've ever seen.
BONNIE	Let's just have a nice glass of champagne and stay calm, and talk this through.
NORRIS	There is absolutely nothing to discuss!
GLEN	(*smiling*) Look, Norris...don't be romantic.
NORRIS	Romantic?
GLEN	Don't be.
NORRIS	I'm not romantic about anything!

BONNIE   You are, you know.

NORRIS   I am not!

NICK   Yes you are, actually.

NORRIS   I'm not!

GLEN   You have romantic notions about children. You have romantic notions about men. And it's clear from the way you're carrying on that you have romantic notions about old people.
Senility and decrepitude obviously suit your picture of a pleasantly oedipal world where no one has to poke their eyes out, no one has to play the profound Freudian farce of sleeping with their mother — or father.
And no one has to lift a finger to kill a parent. No...all you have to do is say their brains are going and shove them — ever so politely — into a hospital or a home. Then plan a nice, ever so romantic funeral.

BONNIE   Glen.

GLEN   Yes?

BONNIE   Don't you think you're being a little strong?

GLEN   Am I?

BONNIE   Yes.

GLEN   Oh. Sorry. Sorry, Norris.

They drink.

BONNIE   Norris wants you to go to Mexico.

GLEN   I hate Mexico.

BONNIE   For laetrile.

GLEN	Oh. (*to* NORRIS) It doesn't work, you know.
NORRIS	(*forced calm, to* NICK) Who do you call when someone is planning to hurt themselves?
NICK	Um...I don't know.
NORRIS	Should I call the police?
BONNIE	You want to have your father arrested?
NICK	They wouldn't do anything.
NORRIS	Why not?
NICK	He hasn't done anything!
NORRIS	Yet!
GLEN	Norris, I am of sound mind, and weak body.
NORRIS	Daddy, this is just horrible.
GLEN	I'm not arguing with that.
NORRIS	What about mother?
GLEN	She's fine.
NORRIS	That's not what I mean.
GLEN	Bonnie? How are you?
BONNIE	I'm fine.
NORRIS	You want him to die?
NICK	Norris...
NORRIS	Do you?

BONNIE	Norris...if you are going to take your parents' deaths personally, you are going to be very unhappy.
NICK	Are you in pain, dad?
NORRIS	That's not the point! (*beat*). The point is, it's not right.
BONNIE	Right?
NORRIS	It's not legal.
GLEN	I didn't say it was.
NORRIS	But you're a lawyer!
GLEN	Retired lawyer. And I'm sorry, but if you want to talk ethics, Norris, there is also nothing to discuss. Ethically, as a dying man, I should have the freedom to choose to die. If you want to drag in morals, or rather, the middle-class morality I suppose we pummelled into you, then you are opening another can of worms entirely. Morally, you could argue that I should not die until I die. Morally, you could say that it is your duty to stop me from taking my own life. Blah. Blah. Ethically, however, I'm sure you find that difficult. Because ethically, you believe that every person has a right to decide their own fate.
NORRIS	I do not.
GLEN	You must. You're my daughter.
NORRIS	But I always think of you as Gregory Peck in *To Kill A Mockingbird.* Aren't you that kind of lawyer?
GLEN	Is that a compliment?
BONNIE	Do you think of every member of your family as someone in a movie?

NORRIS   No!

BONNIE   You called your brother Aunty Mame a little
            while ago.

NORRIS   I did not!

GLEN   You kids thought that movie was about a little
            girl dressed up as a ham and a retarded man called
            Boo Radly who scared her. I think you were
            sixteen before you figured out who Gregory Peck
            was defending.

NORRIS   So? I knew he was good.

GLEN   So was I Norry. But as a defence lawyer, I put a
            lot of riff raf back on the street. And so would
            Gregory Peck, if he'd kept up his practice.

NORRIS   So?

GLEN   Life is simple, Norry. Not simplistic.

NORRIS   You're making fun of me.

GLEN   Well, don't take everything so seriously.

                 The doorbell sounds.

BONNIE   That must be Guy.

GLEN   I'll get it.

                 GLEN *exits.*

BONNIE   He's just in time.

NORRIS   Just in time for what?

NICK   Should he be in the hospital?

BONNIE
I don't remember the last time we had champagne other than New Years. But then that was at Betty Tyler's, so it was probably sparkling wine. She said she wrapped the bottles in tin foil because it was festive, but it was more fizz than bubble if you ask me.

They don't allow champagne in the hospital, you know. All those needles and things, but no champagne.

NORRIS
(*to* NICK) Should he be in the hospital?

BONNIE
This tastes quite good, doesn't it?

NORRIS
I think you've both gone crazy.

BONNIE
Glen warned me you'd feel that way. And it's not that I blame you. I might even be a little hurt, or rather, your father might be a little hurt if you didn't make a fuss. But the point is, as you will discover, after a certain age, we all run the risk of being called crazy.

GUY *enters, followed by* GLEN.

GUY
Hi everyone.

BONNIE
Oh, hello Guy. How are you?

GUY
Fine, thanks.

BONNIE
We expected you for dinner. Nick saved you a piece of pie, but I think he also ate it.

NICK
I did not.

GUY
That's O.K. They always have donuts.

BONNIE
Oh, that's nice. (*beat*). Who does?

GUY
Whoever's turn it is to set up.

BONNIE	Set up what?
GUY	The meeting.
BONNIE	I thought you were working.

GUY *looks at* NICK.

BONNIE	Oh, never mind.

Pause.

BONNIE	How was the drive?
GUY	I took the train.
NORRIS	Guy lost his license, remember?
NICK	I've got the car.
BONNIE	Oh, of course you have.

Pause.

BONNIE	How was the train?
GUY	Fine.

Pause.

BONNIE	Did you walk from the station, then?
GUY	Yes.

Pause.

BONNIE	And how was that?
GLEN	Fine.

BONNIE	How do you know?
GLEN	What else is he going to say, Bonnie?
GUY	It was a nice walk. A little cold maybe.
BONNIE	Does it still smell out there?
GUY	Yeah. What is that?
NICK	A skunk.
GUY	Really?
BONNIE	Haven't you ever smelled a skunk before?
GUY	I guess not. I don't leave the city much.
BONNIE	You haven't, really. We're still considered city in the suburbs.
GLEN	Champagne?
GUY	Uh. No. No thanks.
GLEN	You're sure?
BONNIE	It's French.
GUY	No thank you.
NICK	Guy's being healthy.
BONNIE	Dr. Meissner said that there was nothing wrong with a glass of wine a day. In fact, he even said it was a good idea.
NORRIS	And look at him.
GUY	Pardon?
BONNIE	He's dead. She was making a joke.
NORRIS	I was not making a joke. I was serious.

BONNIE	You know, there is no need to be morbid about all of this.
GUY	It's all right. I really don't want anything to drink.
BONNIE	Just a glass?
NICK	He doesn't want any.
GLEN	How about a brandy?
GUY	No. Thanks.
GLEN	Positive?
GUY	Very.
BONNIE	Can't I get you anything?
GUY	I wouldn't mind some coffee.
BONNIE	That's not very healthy.
GUY	Just a cup.
BONNIE	Well there's some left in the thermos, I suppose.
NICK	I'll get it.

NICK *exits to kitchen.*

BONNIE	But won't that keep you up? Awake, I mean.
GUY	No. It doesn't.
BONNIE	Everybody's different, I guess.
NORRIS	Mother!
BONNIE	What?
NORRIS	Nothing.

BONNIE	What?
GLEN	Your daughter thinks you're making innuendos.
BONNIE	Pooh.
NORRIS	I didn't say anything.
GLEN	You scowled.
NICK	(*calling from kitchen*) Guy! Come in here a minute.
GUY	Excuse me.
BONNIE	He's going to fill you in, I guess. (*beat*) I mean tell you what's going on.

GUY *exits.*

NORRIS	Does Nick give Guy money?
BONNIE	Norris.
NORRIS	It's a legitimate question.
GLEN	Ask them.
BONNIE	Who cares?
NORRIS	I do.
BONNIE	Did he say who had donuts?
NORRIS	No. There was something going on.
BONNIE	You don't know that.
NORRIS	He "looked" at Nick.
BONNIE	Well they do live together.
NORRIS	And he's not bubbling.

GLEN	Pardon?
NORRIS	He always bubbles.
BONNIE	Effusive.
GLEN	Oh.
NORRIS	And I've never seen him refuse a drink before. He's worse than Kevin.
BONNIE	Honestly Norris, he just looked at Nick.
NORRIS	He looked funny.
BONNIE	He always looks funny.
GLEN	He always wears the same pants.
BONNIE	Of course he does. He's a painter.
GLEN	So?
BONNIE	He's supposed to be dirty.
GLEN	No wonder your daughter has romantic notions about everything.
NORRIS	I don't believe this.
GLEN	Believe what?
BONNIE	Disbelief is first. (*to* GLEN) Or is it denial?
GLEN	Denial.
BONNIE	You're in denial Norris.
NORRIS	I'm not denying anything.
BONNIE	You are, you know.

GLEN *starts to exit.*

NORRIS   Where are you going?

GLEN   The bathroom.

NORRIS   Why?

GLEN   Why?

NORRIS   What are you going to do there?

GLEN   Something I have been doing on my own for sixty-five years.

GLEN *exits.*

NORRIS   I'm shaking.

BONNIE   Anger is the turn-around point.

NORRIS   I feel like Anne Bancroft in that movie that was on pay T.V. last week.

BONNIE   I don't know if it's good or it's bad that you keep reducing everything to something else that didn't really happen. I mean, it's fine for now, but...

NORRIS   You don't even know what movie I'm talking about.

BONNIE   It doesn't matter.

NORRIS   It does too.

BONNIE   Fine.

NORRIS   Guy will know what it is.

BONNIE   Just because Guy is a homosexual doesn't mean that he knows the title of every movie that was ever made.

NORRIS	You're horrible.
BONNIE	What about God?
NORRIS	What about God?
BONNIE	Do you think he's Charlton Heston?
NORRIS	No
BONNIE	Who knows...Maybe we should have taken you to church longer.
NORRIS	Maybe you should have.
BONNIE	Maybe it was the luck of the draw, but I've yet to meet a minister with half the bedside manner of a good doctor.
NORRIS	At least we take the boys to church.
BONNIE	I took you too, for a while. You didn't want to go anymore, remember? I respected you. Was I wrong?
NORRIS	Oh please.

NICK *and* GUY *enter from the kitchen.*

BONNIE	Did you get some coffee?
GUY	Yes, thanks.
BONNIE	Is everything all right?
NICK	Why?
BONNIE	Norris thought you looked at Guy.
NICK	What?
BONNIE	Never mind. I didn't think so.

NORRIS	Mother!
BONNIE	You think he's acting?
NICK	Where's dad?
NORRIS	(*significantly, to* NICK) Dad's gone to the bathroom.

> *They all look towards the bathroom, except* BONNIE

BONNIE	Do you remember when you were in the nativity play at the church Nick?
NICK	Pardon?
BONNIE	You were the littlest shepherd. — who's been gathering sticks in the desert to light a fire to warm the holy family. (*to* GUY) He had a little bundle on his shoulder. He was so cute. Anyway, he arrived at the very end of the procession — after thc gold, the myhrr and the frankincense and whatever else Twentieth Century Protestants considered appropriate props — and he goes to look at the baby Jesus in the cradle and what happens when he bends over but all the sticks fall out of the bundle — splat on Jesus. And you know what the worst of it was? No one laughed. Glen and I bit holes in our tongues.
NORRIS	I wish he'd hurry up.
BONNIE	Why?
NORRIS	Because I do.

> *Pause. They all look towards the bathroom, except* BONNIE.

BONNIE	Do you remember that, Nicky?

NICK	The woman who played the King of Myhrr told me I was going to go to hell for what I did to Jesus.
NORRIS	The king is a man.
NICK	Maybe they didn't have enough sensitive men like Kevin to go around in those days.
BONNIE	If I'd known that she told you that, I would have told *her* to go to hell. Why didn't you tell me?
NICK	She was the Sunday school teacher. Mrs. McCardle.
BONNIE	Oh her. I didn't like her at all. (*to* GUY) She tore up Nick's attendance card from Sunday School when he got the measles and chicken pox one after the other and we kept him home for six Sundays in a row. She ripped it up in his face and said "this is what God thinks of you." Can you imagine? As if she'd know what God thought. She probably hadn't even thought about whether or not God thinks. She probably couldn't even think that thought. (*to* NICK) But you didn't cry though, did you, Nicky?
NORRIS	Probably.
BONNIE	No, he didn't.
NICK	I think I'd already started thinking about God like Santa Claus by then, anyway.
BONNIE	Is that what you think of God? Santa Claus?
NICK	I wanted to believe in him...
BONNIE	I suppose Santa Claus is no worse than Charlton Heston.

NICK	I figured that if God was so small as to really care about me missing Sunday school and so stupid as not to have known that I had the measles, that he couldn't be so great after all. He didn't even give presents.
BONNIE	(*to* NORRIS) You were an angel in the nativity play, Norris. We made that silly halo for you out of a wire hanger.(*to* GUY) It bobbed up and down when she walked.
NORRIS	I got my picture in the paper.
BONNIE	You were part of Gabriel's train — Mr. Coates — who got arrested a while ago, by the way, for doing something horrible with a couple of girls on a church outing. He didn't do anything to you, did he?
NORRIS	No!
BONNIE	Good. We all felt terrible at bridge when it happened. I mean all our children are grown up and none of them were molested, which means that some of them probably were, only we don't know about it. (*beat*) The nicest thing about having grown-up children making mistakes of their own is that it alleviates a little of the guilt.
NORRIS	What mistakes?
BONNIE	You'll see.
NORRIS	See what?
BONNIE	Don't take the sins of your mother too serioulsy, that's all.
GUY	Is Glen all right? I mean — now.
BONNIE	He just went to the bathroom.
GUY	But is he "all right"?

NORRIS	He's not doing something is he?
BONNIE	That's a cryptic question.
NORRIS	I think you're exhibiting some kind of pathology.(*to* GUY) Don't you think so, Guy?
BONNIE	Pathology?
NORRIS	You're as cold about this as if it were someone else you were talking about!
	There is a loud bang in the hallway.
NORRIS	Oh my God. He's thrown himself down the stairs!
	NORRIS *runs out, followed by* NICK *and* GUY.
BONNIE	Glen, what are you up to?
NORRIS	(*off*) What was that noise?
GUY	(*off*) Are you O.K.?
NICK	(*off*) What is this?
GLEN	(*off*) It's a box. It was too heavy to carry, so I pushed it.
NORRIS	(*off*) You scared me half to....(*stopping herself*)
BONNIE	Would you all mind coming in here to talk? Glen shouldn't be in that draft. And I don't feel like moving. The champagne has gone to my feet.
GLEN	(*off*) Carry that, would you?
	GLEN *enters the livingroom followed by* NICK, NORRIS *and* GUY — *carrying a large box.*

BONNIE	What was that all about?
GLEN	The box.
BONNIE	Oh.
NORRIS	What's this box for?
GLEN	Just set it down Guy. Thanks.
NICK	What's in it?
GUY	It weighs a ton.
NORRIS	What's in it?
GLEN	Just drop it.
BONNIE	Careful.
NORRIS	What's in it?
GLEN	Evidence.
GUY	Evidence?
NICK	What kind of evidence?
NORRIS	What do you mean "evidence"?
BONNIE	Things.
NORRIS	Things? What kind of things?
GLEN	Anything.
NICK	Do you mean evidence evidence?

GLEN *opens the box.*

GLEN	I mean whatever you want. It's just a box full of things.

NORRIS	(*looking in*) There's a bundle of sticks. What's a bundle of sticks doing in here? What is this?
BONNIE	They're Nick's sticks. That sounds funny, doesn't it? Nick's sticks.
NICK	My sticks.
BONNIE	From Jesus.
NORRIS	From Jesus?
BONNIE	The play. (*to* NORRIS) Your halo's in there too.
NICK	(*pointing at box*) Is this why you brought that up?
BONNIE	Yes. (*to* GLEN) I was talking to Norris about church, then sticks just came into my head. I mean Jesus did, and then sticks. It was associative. (*smiling*)
NORRIS	Hey! Isn't this mine? (*pulling out a little book*) This is my diary! What are you doing with my diary?
BONNIE	We have all sorts of your things in this house that you haven't bothered to move out.
NORRIS	But this is my diary!
GLEN	So?
NORRIS	You shouldn't read my diary.
GLEN	Who said we did?
BONNIE	You were only thirteen. The only thing you wrote about was boys. And that horrible Wendy girl who told on you when you kissed Chris what's-his-name and pretended to put his penis in your mouth.

NORRIS   I did not!

BONNIE   I said you pretended.

NORRIS   Chris who?

BONNIE   God knows. It's all in code in the best bits. He didn't live in this neighbourhood very long. Chris What's-it. I wonder what ever happened to him?

GLEN   Chris who?

NICK   Edelbrock?

BONNIE   That's right! How on earth did you remember that?

GLEN   Chris Edelbrock?

BONNIE   You remember. The one with the chemistry set who set fire to the side of the garage with a bunsen burner.

GUY   I thought Nick did that.

GLEN   What?

NICK   Guy!

BONNIE   Did you do that Nick?

NORRIS   I remember that. (*to* NICK) You blamed it on Chris Thing-me, didn't you?

NICK   We weren't allowed to speak to him anyhow.

NORRIS   Weren't we?

NICK   I never knew why. Was Norris why?

NORRIS   What do you mean?

NICK   I never knew why. Was Norris why?

NORRIS   What do you mean?

NICK   Did you know then that she pretended to put
                Chris Edelbrocks's penis in her mouth?

NORRIS   I didn't!

BONNIE   Oh really. Let's drop Chris What's-it's penis if
                you don't mind!

NORRIS   Please.

BONNIE   It's all a blur now anyway. Whoever he was,
                where ever he ended up, whatever became of him.
                If only he'd had red hair I might remember what
                he looked like. I wonder if he's even alive.

NORRIS   He's my age!

BONNIE   That doesn't mean he's alive.

NORRIS   How do you know that?

BONNIE   I don't, of course. But I'm better off thinking that
                he could be dead than insisting that he isn't.

NORRIS   How can you be so cold?

BONNIE   What do you want me to say?

NORRIS   I don't know!

BONNIE   Honey, I'm not sure at what point my emotional
                detachment began. I mean, I'm sure that I do look
                cold...about..things. But...I don't really know
                what I think I feel anymore — because I know I
                "think" I feel and maybe I don't. Feel.

                It all gets so clouded over the years...words
                started losing their sting at some point in time,
                you know...in your lifetime...In my lifetime too,
                for that matter....God knows when...you could

BONNIE   (*continued*) talking about it sounds muddy
because my thoughts are muddy and my thoughts
are muddy because I can't say what I mean.
Because we don't think the way we used to
anymore. I mean caring about what words really
mean. What they do...well, we just don't think
like that, anymore.

We're cold. Cold-er.

Not that it matters now. Because it doesn't. It —
this — just happened. Like everything just
happens.

So what if Nick almost burned down the garage
and I thought it was Chris Thing-me all these
years? I already hated that kid because of what he
tried to do to Norris in the Thomases storm
cellar. Fellatio.

Remember that word? What is it now? Why am I
pretending I don't know? Blow job.

That's the word, isn't it? The term.
When a woman takes a man's penis in her
mouth. Or a man does. Like my son. Who does
that. I mean I know he does, whether or not I
like to think he does. Knowing and thinking are
very different things, aren't they? And if we
think about it, we know a hell of a lot more than
we want to. Don't we? Who cares, of course.

Everybody's got a bubble in them, Dr. Meissner
says. Said. And it can only take up so much
room before it forces whatever we are — out. So
now when he's asleep and I'm not, I lie there and
think that Glen's got a bubble in him.
A bubble like in double bubble bubble gum, just
waiting for God to blow into it. Is God like that?

Is God that banal?

BONNIE   (*continued*) pick any date in this century and it
wouldn't matter...but you see, our ability to feel
anything is bound to our ability to express it and
my talking about it sounds muddy because my
thoughts are muddy and my thoughts are muddy
because I can't say what I mean. Because we don't
think the way we used to anymore. I mean caring
about what words really mean. What they
do...well, we just don't think like that, anymore.

We're cold. Cold-er.

Not that it matters now. Because it doesn't. It
—this — just happened. Like everything just
happens.

So what if Nick almost burned down the garage
and I thought it was Chris Thing-me all these
years? I already hated that kid because of what he
tried to do to Norris in the Thomases storm
cellar. Fellatio.

Remember that word? What is it now? Why am I
pretending I don't know? Blow job.

That's the word, isn't it? The term.
When a woman takes a man's penis in her
mouth. Or a man does. Like my son. Who does
that. I mean I know he does, whether or not I
like to think he does. Knowing and thinking are
very different things, aren't they? And if we
think about it, we know a hell of a lot more than
we want to. Don't we? Who cares, of course.

Everybody's got a bubble in them, Dr. Meissner
says. Said. And it can only take up so much
room before it forces whatever we are — out. So
now when he's asleep and I'm not, I lie there and
think that Glen's got a bubble in him.
A bubble like in double bubble bubble gum, just
waiting for God to blow into it. Is God like that?

Is God that banal?

BONNIE   (*continued*) When I think about it in those terms I have to put the other God out of my mind. You know, the God like the painting in the Sistine Chapel.

Big God, little man. Painted by a man who took a man's penis in his mouth at the behest of a pope. (*beat*)

The painting was a behest I mean.

But it does make you think, doesn't it?

I mean I look at all those women on the news with veils on their faces and all those black clothes in the hundred degree heat and their husbands beating themselves with chains and I have to really wonder what anything means. I mean, is that what's going on in the world while I'm at the grocery store looking for a roast to serve my family before we tell them that their father's going to die and their mother's selling everything and going to Tibet?

                     Pause.

GLEN   You know, with Kevin not here, this may not be fair.

BONNIE   Now that's a good old-fashioned word now, isn't it? Fair.

NORRIS   What do you mean "old-fashioned"?

NICK   What do you mean "fair"?

GLEN   (*to* NORRIS) Anachronistic. (*to* NICK) Equitable.

BONNIE   (*to* GLEN) Does all knowledge become esoteric?

GLEN   Probably.

BONNIE	Really?
GLEN	Everything is eking towards banality.
BONNIE	Is that cold, Norris?
NORRIS	Yes.
BONNIE	You know, maybe what you call cold is just profound cynicism.
NORRIS	There's nothing profound about cynicism.
GLEN	No?
NORRIS	I think you're both crazy.
GLEN	We're both old.
NORRIS	That has nothing to do with it. Phoebe McCarthy's parents are both older than you and they're not crazy. They've got a nice condo in Fort Lauderdale.
BONNIE	Do they?
NORRIS	Why can't *you* get a condo in Fort Lauderdale?
BONNIE	I don't want a condo in Fort Lauderdale! I want to wear a sari on top of a mountain and rub tiger balm on my forehead and eat yak yogurt and meet Richard Burton in *The Rains of Ranchipur*.
GLEN	You do?
BONNIE	Only when you're dead, darling.
GLEN	Oh.
NORRIS	Is that supposed to make him feel better?
BONNIE	(*to* GLEN) Doesn't it?

GLEN	I suppose so.
NICK	(*to* NORRIS) Richard Burton's dead anyway.
BONNIE	So?
NORRIS	He was an alcoholic.
BONNIE	Was he?
GUY	(*quickly*) I'm an alcoholic.

Beat.

BONNIE	There's still some champagne left. (*beat*) I mean, not that you want any.
GUY	Nick's embarrassed.
NORRIS	Nick's an alcoholic.
NICK	Oh shut up.
NORRIS	So's Kevin.
BONNIE	Is he?
NORRIS	He was drunk on our first date.
BONNIE	Was he?
NORRIS	Was dad?
BONNIE	We went bowling.
NORRIS	Was he an alcoholic?
GLEN	I've slipped into past tense already.
NORRIS	I mean were you. Before.
GLEN	Before what?

NORRIS	I don't know. Before I remember. When I was a kid. Were you?
GUY	I joined A.A.
BONNIE	Oh?
GLEN	No. I wasn't. Why?
GUY	(*proudly*) I attended my first meeting tonight.
BONNIE	Oh.
NORRIS	I'm looking for a pattern in my life.
GLEN	Why?
NORRIS	Because it's a mess!
GUY	(*to* NORRIS, *helpfully*) Maybe you should join.
NORRIS	I'm not an alcoholic. You're the alcoholic. You're the one who blacks out at parties and stays awake at the same time and jumps into people's jacuzzi's with your clothes on and sounds sober right up until you conk out.

Beat.

GUY	Thank you.
NORRIS	What?
NICK	Thank her for what?
GUY	For reminding me.
NICK	Reminding you of what?
GUY	I don't know. I mean that's why I'm glad to be told. So I can make amends.
NORRIS	Amends?

GLEN	What do you care about a pattern in your life? What pattern?
NORRIS	This!
GLEN	This what?
BONNIE	Yes, this what, honey?
NORRIS	You!
GLEN	Me?
BONNIE	Him?
NORRIS	No.
BONNIE	He didn't molest you.
NORRIS	You!
GLEN	Her?
BONNIE	Me?
NORRIS	Yes!
BONNIE	What have I done?
NORRIS	Nothing!
GLEN	Don't shout at your mother.
BONNIE	She can if she wants to. But I don't know what she's shouting about.
NORRIS	Nothing!
GLEN	Well what are you shouting about nothing for?
GUY	Angst?
GLEN	What angst?

NORRIS	Shut up! Just shut up! Please.

Pause.

BONNIE	Angst is a good word. (*beat*) Don't you think?
NORRIS	No.
BONNIE	We should use it more often. It's very apt. (*beat*) Apt's a good word too. Don't you think?
NORRIS	No.
BONNIE	Glen?
GLEN	Depends.
GUY	(*to* NORRIS) Are you O.K.?
NORRIS	Now he's solicitous.
GUY	What's wrong?
NORRIS	Nothing.
GLEN	Nothing?
NICK	Nothing.
BONNIE	You don't mean *nothing* do you?
NORRIS	Yes I do mean nothing!

Punched in my head kind of nothing that I get all the time with my migraines. Just sitting around the laundromat kind of nothing that I have had all my life. Losing socks and hiding the stains in my bikini pants and Kevin's shorts by folding them the right way on top of the basket because I'm afraid people might see and think I don't care.

I mean that stupid nothing...

them the right way on top of the basket because
I'm afraid people might see and think I don't care.

I mean that stupid nothing...

NORRIS   (*continued*) The nothing I get when Kevin goes
out on Thursday night — every Thursday — and
I turn on the television and see things I don't
believe and still have to give over to because if I
didn't I would go into the kitchen and eat all of
the Oreo cookies and the polish sausages Kevin's
mother gives us and he hates. The nothing like
the middle of Friday afternoon nothing when I
have had four cups of coffee and I feel so tired
that I don't care if I sell anymore typewriters, but
I know that if I don't we won't get the mortgage
paid until I'm sixty and by then I won't want to
go to Egypt and sit on a stinking camel and have
my picture taken with travel guides the way you
have and I'm jealous of. Don't you see what I
mean?

Like just the fact that I'm having another baby
and want it and don't want it and the fact that I'm
having a divorce and I want it and don't want it
and the fact that I already have two kids that I
want and don't want and Nick always being in the
paper and being so smug about it and Kevin
drinking and now Guy being a drunk. Alcoholic,
sorry. Guy being an alcoholic and not
remembering — not that I really thought he
would — that he's the father. Maybe.

Long pause.

GLEN   Well, I don't know about you, but,
philosophically speaking, I think it's kind of nice
to know that in the grand scheme of things, my
death becomes less significant everytime
someone opens their mouth.

BONNIE   What?

NICK	Norris, are you serious?

> NORRIS *looks at* GUY.

NICK	(*to* GUY) Is she?
GUY	(*to* NORRIS) Are you?
NORRIS	Guess.
NICK	Norris!
BONNIE	Norris, I think this is just a little too complicated to leave hanging in the air. Don't you?
NICK	Guy, is this true?
GUY	I don't know.
NICK	Just cause you can't remember doesn't mean you could forget something like this.With Norris? I mean, could you?
GUY	I don't know.
NORRIS	What's that supposed to mean?
BONNIE	Norris stay out of it.
NORRIS	What do you mean stay out of it? I am it.
NICK	Stay out of it.
NORRIS	Are you finally jealous of me?
GLEN	I don't think I can die now.
BONNIE	Oh Glen, really?
GLEN	I mean *now*. What's going to happen?
NORRIS	It's none of your business.

BONNIE	Norris!
NORRIS	Well it's not. It's my business.
GLEN	The bubble.
BONNIE	The bubble?
GUY	Norris...It just doesn't, you know, even in my wildest fantasies, it's just not even one of my fantasies...I don't like you. I'm sorry.
NICK	(*to* NORRIS) How many candidates are there?
BONNIE	Nick...
NICK	Can you count them on one hand?
GUY	Was this — did this, if it did happen, happen?
BONNIE	Nick...
GLEN	It's so..."oh".
BONNIE	Oh?
NORRIS	What?
GLEN	...Did?...

GLEN *slumps over in his chair.*

BONNIE	Glen?
NORRIS	Oh my God. What's he done?
NICK	Dad?
GUY	Glen?
BONNIE	Honey?
NORRIS	Is he all right?

GUY	Glen?
BONNIE	Honey?
NORRIS	Is he all right?
NICK	(*approaching him*) Dad?
NORRIS	What's the matter?
NICK	Dad?
GUY	Should I call an ambulance?
BONNIE	I don't know.
NORRIS	Yes!
NICK	Dad?
GUY	Is it my fault?
BONNIE	I don't know.
NORRIS	Yes.
NICK	Dad?
GUY	I'll call an ambulance.

> GUY *exits.* NICK *checks* GLEN's *pulse.* NORRIS *watches in horror.* BONNIE *rises and goes to the box.*

BONNIE	Well?
NORRIS	Is he...?
NICK	I don't know...
BONNIE	He wanted you to have all these things. They are your things of course. Things we gave you. He gave you. And I suppose you cared about once.

NORRIS   Is he...?

BONNIE   I'm glad you remembered Chris-what's-his-name's name. Neither one of us could. It was driving me crazy.

NORRIS   I have to sit down.

BONNIE   We were afraid you were going to fight over some of these things so we wanted you both to be with your, well, your combine. Of course we didn't know anything about...Well. Now we do. I do.

Who wants the Winnie the Pooh books?

NORRIS   The twins should have them.

BONNIE   Nick?

NICK   I don't care.

BONNIE   Catch.

                    BONNIE *throws four books at* NORRIS.

NORRIS   (*quitetly*) Mother. Stop it.

BONNIE   I suppose Nick should get the field glasses then.

NORRIS   ...The twins should get them.

NICK   He's dead. (*pause*) I can't feel any pulse.

BONNIE   Glen?

                    GUY *enters.*

GUY   I called an ambulance.

BONNIE   Really? I'm glad he's not dying then. He'd be
dead by the time they got here.

Pause.

NORRIS   Should I call Kevin?

BONNIE   Wouldn't it be funny if he died of natural causes?
Well it wouldn't be "funny", but it would be
funny. Wouldn't it?

Are you crying, Norris?

I suppose it would be fair to say that I'm in shock.
Not that I'm incoherent. I know what I'm saying.
After all, I'm prepared for this. Well, not this
specifically, but this generally. I'm only surprised,
of course, because at least if he had killed himself, I
would have been able to say what I wanted to say.

Like in the movies, Norris. (*beat*)

In India, a good wife jumps on her husband's
funeral pyre. Here, a good wife sends his clothes
to the Salvation Army and doesn't date for at
least three months. (*beat*)

If he were a Pharaoh, though, I'd be buried alive
with him in his pyramid to cook his breakfast on
the other side. But that's only marginally more
civil than jumping on his pyre if you ask me.
Which of course you wouldn't, because it
wouldn't be right. And we're all alright here.

At least, though, that way there's some resolution.
So you're not just hanging there — in grief, in
love, in shock — confused —whatever — thinking
about it...hoping some convention will hold you in
check until it's over, and then wondering if it really
was the end. Is the end. "The end," like in your
movie, Norris. The end.

Fade to Black.